THIS BOOK BELONGS TO

_____

FOR ALL THE YOUNG DREAMERS
AND CURIOUS SOULS.

❖

Running Press Kids
Hachette Book Group
1290 Avenue of the Americas, New York, NY 10104
www.runningpress.com/rpkids
@runningpresskids

Distributed in the United Kingdom by Little, Brown Book Group UK,
Carmelite House, 50 Victoria Embankment, London, EC4Y 0DZ

First Edition: September 2024

Published by Running Press Kids, an imprint of Hachette Book Group, Inc.
The Running Press Kids name and logo are trademarks of Hachette Book Group, Inc.

The Hachette Speakers Bureau provides a wide range of authors for speaking events. To find out more, go to www.hachettespeakersbureau.com or email HachetteSpeakers@hbgusa.com.

Running Press books may be purchased in bulk for business, educational, or promotional use. For more information, please contact your local bookseller or the Hachette Book Group Special Markets Department at Special.Markets@hbgusa.com.

The publisher is not responsible for websites (or their content) that are not owned by the publisher.

Print book cover and interior design by Mary Boyer.

Library of Congress Cataloging-in-Publication Data
Names: Van De Car, Nikki, author. | Kita, Kiki, illustrator.
Title: My Wheel of the Year: a celebration of nature's magic/
written by Nikki Van De Car; illustrated by Kiki Kita.
Description: First Edition. | Philadelphia, PA: Running Press, [2024] | Audience: Ages 4-8 years | Summary: "A mystical picture book celebrating the eight Pagan festivals that make up the Wheel of the Year"—Provided by publisher.
Identifiers: LCCN 2023010538 (print) | ISBN 9780762485277 (hardcover)
Subjects: LCSH: Festivals—Juvenile literature. | Holidays—Juvenile literature. | Neopaganism—Rituals—Juvenile literature. | Paganism—Juvenile literature. | Sabbat—Juvenile literature.
Classification: LCC GT3933 .V356 2024 (print) | DDC 394.26—dc23/eng/20231030
LC record available at https://lccn.loc.gov/2023010538

ISBN: 978-0-7624-8527-7

Printed in China

APS

10 9 8 7 6 5 4 3 2 1

MY WHEEL OF THE YEAR

A CELEBRATION OF
NATURE'S MAGIC

Nikki Van De Car

Illustrated by **Kiki Kita**

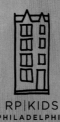

RP|KIDS
PHILADELPHIA

As the earth goes around the sun, the seasons change. Year after year. On and on and on, round and round. Spring brings warmth and life to Summer, which brings heat and growth to Autumn, which brings harvest and cold to Winter, which brings rest and rebirth to Spring.

This cycle is known as the Wheel of the Year. There is joy in this
endless turning, in the certainty that nothing ever ends but is only reborn.

Within the Wheel are eight spokes, which represent eight holidays. These holidays mark the different seasons and have been celebrated by various cultures around the world for thousands of years, though they have a lot of different names depending on where in the world you are—but in witchy, pagan culture they are known as Sabbats.

YULE
DECEMBER 20-23

SAMHAIN
NOVEMBER 1

IMBOLC
FEBRUARY 1

MABON
SEPTEMBER 21-24

OSTARA
MARCH 19-22

LUGHNASADH
AUGUST 1

BELTANE
MAY 1

LITHA
JUNE 19-23

SAMHAIN
(SOW-in)
OCTOBER 31

According to traditions of the Wheel, the year begins not on January 1, but on October 31, called Samhain—which you likely know as Halloween. In fact, Halloween is based on the celebrations of Samhain! On this night, as we celebrate the start of a new year, we say goodbye to the old one.

RITUAL FOR SAMHAIN

Going trick-or-treating is a great way to celebrate Samhain.
You can also bury some apples for any lost spirits who may be wandering,
or light some candles in your windows to invite your ancestors to come visit.

YULE

(YEW-ell)

DECEMBER 20 OR 21

Yule falls on the Winter Solstice, also known as the longest night of the year. It is the night when the earth is farthest from the sun, and it means that even though Winter has arrived, every night from here on out will be shorter, and every day will be longer.

There's a legend that says that on the night of Yule, the Holly King, the lord of Winter, defeats the Oak King, the lord of Spring, allowing all the animals (and people!) to rest safely and peacefully over the Winter months.

RITUAL FOR YULE

Gather together with your family by a window. At the exact moment
the sun goes down, make a wish for what the next year will bring for you.

IMBOLC
(IM-blk)
ON OR AROUND FEBRUARY 2

Imbolc means that Winter is nearly over!
It's time to start preparing for the coming Spring.

Imbolc is often also a celebration of Brighid (Breej),
the Celtic goddess of fire, healing, and poetry.

RITUAL FOR IMBOLC

Celebrate with your family by reading poems together by candlelight or by going out for a walk in the chill air, searching for early signs of Spring like crocuses, snowdrops, or daffodils.

OSTARA
(oh-STAH-rah)
ON OR AROUND MARCH 20

Ostara falls on the Spring Equinox, when the length of the day
is equal to the length of the night. As the first official day
of Spring, it's a day of balance and of welcoming the new life.

RITUAL FOR OSTARA

You can celebrate by working in the earth,
tending to the new plants—either in your own garden,
or in a community garden, or even in the park or the woods!

BELTANE
(BAY-al-TIN-uh)

MAY 1

The most joyful of holidays falls at the height of Spring. It is a celebration of life and of all that makes us happy. Beltane means "bright fire," and one of the ways people have traditionally celebrated is to light a bonfire and dance around it. This holiday is about playing and having fun, so simply running around outside with friends/family is a wonderful way to celebrate.

RITUAL FOR BELTANE

Splash wild water on your face—wild water means anything
that doesn't come from a faucet, so it can be rainwater or water
from a stream, or even water collected from dew on the grass.

LITHA

(LIE-tha)

ON OR AROUND JUNE 21

Litha, also known as the Summer Solstice, marks the longest day of the year. On this day, the sun is closest to the Earth, and Summer has truly begun. Of course, this also means that from here on out, the days will be shorter, and the nights will be longer.

Litha is the day the Oak King, the lord of Summer, defeats the Holly King, and rules over the world for the remaining half of the year.

RITUAL FOR LITHA

Wake up early to watch the sunrise and greet the dawn by listing
all you are grateful for, as you welcome the time of the Oak King.

LAMMAS
(Luh-MAHS)
AUGUST 1–2

Lammas marks the first harvest of the year, when the first growing crops are ready to eat. Long ago, before grocery stores, our lives were ruled by when our food was finished growing, so this first harvest was really important! We celebrate it to remember all that our ancestors did to give us the lives we have now.

RITUAL FOR LAMMAS

Lammas means "loaf-mass" because long ago, people would place loaves of bread on altars to honor the Sun God. Lammas is celebrated at the same time as "Lugnasadh" (LOO-nuh-suh), a day when the god Lugh held sporting events like the Olympics in honor of his mother. You could gather friends and family to play games outside and then make your own bread to eat!

MABON
(MAY-bun)
ON OR AROUND SEPTEMBER 21

The final holiday of the Wheel of the Year falls on the
Autumn Equinox. Just like Ostara, it's a time of balance,
as the length of the day is equal to the length of the night.
From here on out, the nights will be longer than the days,
as the power of the Holly King grows.

Mabon is also a time of harvest, but it is nearing the end of
the season, as we prepare for our time of rest. It's a night for
expressing your gratitude for all that you have been given,
and for remembering that as this turn of the Wheel comes
to a close, it will go right around again. As the leaves
begin to fall and the animals go into hibernation,
remember that they will awaken again.

RITUAL FOR MABON

Read aloud legends and stories of cycles and rebirth,
like Persephone, Osiris, and Jesus Christ.

Celebrating these holidays is a way of connecting with nature and the magic of the earth.
We carry the power of the earth within us, and each of these holidays is a reminder of this truth:

YOU ARE FULL OF MAGIC.

CRAFTS TO HONOR THE FESTIVALS

As you celebrate the various holidays, try some
of these crafts with your family and friends!

SAMHAIN:

Make a protective charm bag to carry with you when you go
trick-or-treating. Cut a four-inch square of cloth and place inside it:

1 obsidian stone • 1 garlic clove • 2–3 holly berries

Pull the corners of the cloth together and tie them tight with a string.

YULE:

Collect a bucket or bag of pinecones. Mix two parts warm water and
one part vinegar and let the pinecones soak for about thirty minutes.
Remove them from the water and allow them to dry for a few hours.
Take a long piece of yarn and string it around the cones
to create a garland—and you could also use them to make
a wreath to hang on your door and welcome Winter.

IMBOLC:

Make a Brighid's Cross by collecting some straw or grass. Weave them
into a square at the center, crossing back and forth, and then tie off the
strands. Hang your cross in your doorway for protection and healing.

OSTARA:

Plant a seed either in the ground if it's warm enough
or in a small pot indoors. It can be a flower, or an herb, or even
something that will one day go on your dinner table—you choose!

BELTANE:

Collect flowers and make a flower crown, and you might even
gather some friends to dance together around a maypole!

LITHA:

We honor the Oak King by eating fresh fruit and celebrating all the light and
energy we are blessed with during this time of the year. Place a lemon or
mandarin orange at the center of a large plate or platter, and then arrange
any other fruit you have around it to symbolize the rays of the sun.

LAMMAS:

Take some fresh-shucked corn leaves from the first corn harvest
and make them into a little doll. You can hang the doll in your room
where she will protect until you make a new one next Lammas!

MABON:

Take a walk outside and gather a few acorns.
When you get home, gently clean them off with warm, soapy water.
Once they've dried, paint them the color of your choice, and then
knot a string around the cap and wear as a pendant for protection.